The Bitcoin King Had No Clothes

Mark Simmons
Satoshi Nakamoto,
Hans Christian Andersen

Once upon a time, in a far-off kingdom, there lived a king who ruled over the world of crypto. This king was known as the Bitcoin King, and he was highly respected by all the people in the kingdom.

He was so fond of new clothes that he spent all his money on them in order to be beautifully dressed.

He did not care about his soldiers; he did not care about his people; he only wanted that all the people in the kingdom – must use Bitcoin as their currency.

One day, the Bitcoin King declared that all the people in the kingdom must use Bitcoin as their currency. And so, everyone started buying and trading Bitcoin, eager to get rich quick.

The kingdom was in a frenzy, with people buying Bitcoin every day.

In the great city in which he lived there was always something going on; every day many strangers came there. One day two impostors arrived who gave themselves out as weavers, and said that they knew how to manufacture the most beautiful cloth imaginable, and if the Bitcoin King wear these clothes more and more people will buy and use this currency…

Not only were the texture and pattern uncommonly beautiful, but the clothes which were made of the stuff possessed this wonderful property that they were invisible to anyone who was not fit for his office, or who was unpardonably stupid.

'Those must indeed be splendid clothes,' thought the Emperor. 'If I had them on I could find out which men in my kingdom are unfit for the offices they hold; I could distinguish the wise from the stupid!

And people that are wise or think that are wise will use Bitcoin as their currency, or think that they can buy Bitcoin as a store of value, even that it doesn't have any value, and they will never use it…

Yes, this cloth must be woven for me at once.

5

And he gave both the impostors much money, so that they – might begin their work.

They placed two weaving-looms, and began to do as if they were working, but they had not the least thing on the looms. In the same way that his idea:

Bitcoin ₿

had nothing to back up his currency

They also demanded the finest silk and the best gold, which they put in their pockets, and worked at the empty looms till late into the night.

'I should like very much to know how far they have got on with the cloth,' thought the Emperor. But he remembered when he thought about it that whoever was stupid or not fit for his office would not be able to see it. Now he certainly believed that he had nothing to fear for himself, but he wanted first to send somebody else in order to see how he stood with regard to his office. Everybody in the whole town knew what a wonderful power the cloth had, and they were all curious to see how bad or how stupid their neighbor was.

I will give interviews thought the Emperor.
"Financial Experts" will speak about my currency,
newspapers, books will write about it's bright future…

and more and more people will buy it…

The impostors now wanted more money, more silk, and more gold to use in their weaving. They put it all in their own pockets, and there came no threads on the loom, but they went on as they had done before, working at the empty loom. The Emperor soon sent another worthy statesman to see how the weaving was getting on, and whether the cloth would soon be finished. It was the same with him as the first one; he looked and looked, but because there was nothing on the empty loom he could see nothing.

'Is it not a beautiful piece of cloth?' asked the two impostors, and they pointed to and described the splendid material which was not there.

'Stupid I am not!' thought the man, 'so it must be my good office for which I am not fitted. It is strange, certainly, but no one must be allowed to notice it.' And so, he praised the cloth which he did not see, and expressed to them his delight at the beautiful colors and the splendid texture. 'Yes, it is quite beautiful,' he said to the Emperor.

Everybody in the town was talking of the magnificent cloth, and how they can get rich quick buying Bitcoin…

Now the Emperor wanted to see it himself while it was still on the loom. With a great crowd of select followers, amongst whom were both the worthy statesmen who had already been here before, he went to the cunning impostors, who were now weaving with all their might, but without fiber or thread.

'Is it not splendid!' said both the old statesmen who had already been there. 'See, your Majesty, what a texture! What colors!

And then they pointed to the empty loom, for they believed that the others could see the cloth quite well.

'What!' thought the Emperor, 'I can see nothing! This is indeed horrible! Am I stupid? Am I not fit to be Emperor? That were the most dreadful thing that could happen to me.

'Oh, it is very beautiful,' he said. 'It has my gracious approval.' And then he nodded pleasantly, and examined the empty loom, for he would not say that he could see nothing.

His whole Court round him looked and looked, and saw no more than the others; but they said like the Emperor, 'Oh! it is beautiful!' And they advised him to wear these new and magnificent clothes for the first time at the great procession which was soon to take place. 'Splendid! Lovely! Most beautiful!' went from mouth to mouth; everyone seemed delighted over them, and the Emperor gave to the impostors the title of Court weavers to the Emperor.

Throughout the whole of the night before the morning on which the procession was to take place, the impostors were up and were working by the light of over sixteen candles. The people could see that they were very busy making the Emperor's new clothes ready.

They pretended they were taking the cloth from the loom, cut with huge scissors in the air, sewed with needles without thread, and then said at last, 'Now the clothes are finished!'

The Emperor came himself with his most distinguished knights, and each impostor held up his arm just as if he were holding something, and said, 'See! here are the breeches! Here is the coat! Here the cloak!' and so on. 'Spun clothes are so comfortable that one would imagine one had nothing on at all; but that is the beauty of it!' 'Yes,' said all the knights, but they could see nothing, for there was nothing there.

'Will it please your Majesty graciously to take off your clothes,' said the impostors, 'then we will put on the new clothes, here before the mirror.'

The Emperor took off all his clothes, and the impostors placed themselves before him as if they were putting on each part of his new clothes which was ready, and the Emperor turned and bent himself in front of the mirror.

'How beautifully they fit! How well they sit!' said everybody. 'What material! What colours! It is a gorgeous suit!'
'They are waiting outside with the canopy which your Majesty is wont to have borne over you in the procession, ' announced the Master of the Ceremonies.
'Look, I am ready,' said the Emperor. 'Doesn't it sit well!' And he turned himself again to the mirror to see if his finery was on all right.

23

The chamberlains who were used to carry the train put their hands near the floor as if they were lifting up the train; then they did as if they were holding something in the air. They would not have it noticed that they could see nothing.

So the Emperor went along in the procession under the splendid canopy, and all the people in the streets and at t he windows said, 'How matchless are the Emperor's new clothes! That train fastened to his dress, how beautifully it hangs!'

No one wished it to be noticed that he could see nothing, for then he would have been unfit for his office, or else very stupid. None of the Emperor's clothes had met with such approval as these had.

'But he has nothing on!' said a little boy.

And he said to the King, "Excuse me, but I think you have no clothes." The crowd gasped in shock as the little boy pointed out that the Bitcoin King had no clothes and in the same way nothing to back up his currency. There was no real value behind Bitcoin, it was just a digital token with no assets to support it.

'Just listen to the innocent child!' said the father, and each one whispered to his neighbour what the child had said.

'But he has nothing on!' and this currency is worthless…

the whole of the people called out at last.

As the truth about Bitcoin spread throughout the kingdom, people began to realize that they had been fooled. They had invested their hard-earned money in something that had no real value.

This struck the Emperor, for it seemed to him as if they
were right.

This struck the Emperor, for it seemed to him as if they were right.

The little boy's bravery and wisdom taught the people of the kingdom an important lesson. Just because something is popular and everyone is doing it, doesn't mean it's a wise investment. It's important to do your research and understand the true value of an investment before putting your money into it.

31

His wisdom lived on, and he was remembered as the one who bravely spoke the truth and saved the people of the kingdom from financial ruin. And so, the story of "The Bitcoin King Had No Clothes" became a cautionary tale for generations to come.

The end.

www.ingramcontent.com/pod-product-compliance
Lightning Source LLC
Chambersburg PA
CBHW052339210326

41597CB00031B/5308